MIND, PAIN, FEELING, HEALING, NEW BEGINNINGS

I0617996

LOIS E. LUND

Mind, Pain, Feeling, Healing, New Beginnings
Copyright © 2023 by Lois E. Lund

ISBN: (Paperback)   978-1959151371
          (e-book)   978-1959151388
          (Hardback)   978-1959151395

The Reading Glass Books
1-888-420-3050
www.readingglassbooks.com
production@readingglassbooks.com

CONTENTS

FOREWORD

This book is for those many people who come to a turning point in their lives; especially those who have chemical imbalances to speak of in their lives. I've had many classes and know the importance of suitable behavior. Even when we're stressed, we need composure.

It is also for those many people who come to a turning point in their life. It is instructional for those who don't understand those who have mental problems. There are increasing numbers of people who have stress and taking a pill is not the worst thing that you might do for some relief. I have waited for 30 years to find the right pill cocktail. I'm bipolar and I need them.

Also, there are methods to find healing. In my bibliography are three resources. I am mostly writing from my personal experience. A lot has been studied about mental illnesses.

I have found comfort in my own way and this is what I've learned.

I am a veteran and I was sick with emotional pain as well as having a chemical imbalance in my brain. This account isn't too long so you won't find big words in it. I want to share my story with you. I hope it helps.

Lois Lund, Author

CHAPTER

1

To be fair, I would like to explain this is for those who are beset by emotional pain and have a disorder of chemical imbalance in our brains. We all have abilities to nurture ourselves after serving our country in the armed forces. As a veteran receiving benefits, I feel I must write. I took the tests and qualified for the Navy. So, in January 1975 I left on a bus to Florida from Iowa for Basic training. We had exercise, marching relay running and several classes. There were protestant classes and Catholic Church. Breakfast, lunch and dinner were provided. We went to the dentist and got haircuts or wore our hair up. Sometimes we would come back to our barracks and our company commander would have our lockers open and our belongings on the floor. She would say our lockers were a mess inside so, you have to stow away your lockers neatly this time. At one point she said I should have a visit with the psychiatrist. I didn't know what was happening with me?! I didn't trust anybody at that point. I didn't know anybody else who had to take medicine but Thyroid.

I went to see him with my fiancé. I told the Dr. I had seen a vision of an angel over a church. I was so miserable I knew the sky was up but not too much more than that. I didn't know right from wrong. The Doctor told my fiancé I was crazy. I was given an honorable discharge. I should have told his commanding officer. That was inappropriate for a doctor to say.

I was so stressed out at that moment; I'll never forget that scene in the sky that afternoon as we drove around the lake. Those with great trauma or stress especially depression might have vision that nobody else could see. I saw an angel in the sky over a big church. In my next job I was in a holding place and worked in x-ray filing x-rays by social security numbers. In Indiana and experiencing the beautiful Queen Ann's Lace plant growing wild and free along the roadsides and ditches in middle America. This Indiana; is where I grew up. The flower blooms out just like a white crochet piece. We had four distinct seasons in Indiana; winter snow and cold, in the spring time to plant summer to maintain your plants and swim and sports then fall. Also, I mowed the yard. In the navy I learned to correct way to brush my teeth. We were measured and our uniforms were tailored made to fit. There is still something about Indiana that I still love. Over cast days. In the fall my hair would shine.

After filing x-rays, I got a job in a navy automotive parts store as a clerk I checked out spark plugs, wiper blades and automotive grease, filters, and etc. After that I ran my own business cleaning houses. I had seven loyal customers at $15.00 dollars an hour part time wasn't too bad. After that I worked for a growing business cleaning service. I was the desk clerk and did learn bookkeeping eventually. I went to school. I was at the office. I learned to do payroll by asking questions. I really liked that job. Eventually I had to take accounting class.

In the Navy my duty station was the Recruit Dispensary working swing shift. I worked with the kids who had "recruit crud". Their blood pressures, pulse, and respirations had to be documented. And I could dispense pills. I had little or no experience to do this. I was doing stuff I had never done before. I was not a natural. I needed more experience. I was supposed to change the IV on a very sick patient, but I didn't know what I was doing. I felt so inadequate. I told the nurse and she was angry with me. She had her boyfriend on the ward with her. Well, I called my boyfriend, but he couldn't get on the base. I went downstairs to try to see him. Of course, he couldn't get on base. So, he called me and told me so.

CHAPTER

2

I was taken over to a bed at the hospital and they gave me a shot of valium. It didn't make me feel better. I was so helpless. I didn't know what was happening to me. I knew I was in trouble and I couldn't pray. That was the worst thing.

I was transferred to Orange Memorial hospital. I was 24 years old. My new home was a 40 ft. by 40 ft… room they took my clothes. And gave me a yellow paper gown. I wasn't cold. I was not hot but I was so sick of heart and mind. I spent the whole weekend there with nobody to see me. I walked, I banged on the door. They finally set me outside the room in a chair with a belt around me. The Dr. didn't see me until Monday morning. He shook his head when he saw me. He asked me some questions then he ordered some medications for me.

The door was scratched and marked up with a ring, I guess. Three days and two nights I was there. I was totally not registering was I ever getting out of there? Was I ever going to feel good again?

How in the world could I help anybody else? One lady prayed for deliverance for me. I didn't know how to pray. I never knew what was next. I didn't want to be sick I didn't know that medication would make me feel better.

As a child I had bad experiences. You must have guidance through this. It is not normal or O.K. to have been molested or not supervised. These are scars that will not go away for in a few weeks. After some time, you have to face your experiences with God or a counsellor or a good listening ear. Eventually you have to have to face the truth even though it hurts. That is what counselors can do. But mostly I came to terms with my situation but I handled it badly honestly. Then after a long time I felt some closure on that. You have to try to forgive them or get someone to listen to you. No matter what, it still happened. Be smarter and 'let- it- go'.

I grew up in a family with four boys and one girl. That was me, Lois.

I, my younger brother and I played outside. I had a good toy silver pistol with a holster and a favorite doll. We would act out things we saw on television. We ran around the house outside like we were riding horses. Zorro was good and Combat was fun. When you were dead, you stopped and counted to 30 with your eyes closed. Then opened them and were back at it. In winter we dug out snow tunnels, made snowmen and snow balls. I was a tomboy. I learned to hit the tennis ball and loved ice skating. What a chump I was. Little Gooey my friends called me in elementary school… I didn't mind it. They took my first name: Lois and attached the first letter of my last name G and made Gooey. It was my nick name. I loved recess. My oldest brother would tease me. He said, "Can you see your feet?" I didn't know what he meant. He was just clowning around. I didn't like any remarks about by body He tried to tell me I was pretty. But I didn't believe him. I felt pretty plain.

You are not plain to God. He made you. You are unique!

In my life I had bad experiences. You have to try to forgive them or get someone to listen to you. No matter what is happening. Be smarter and 'let-it-go." I am bipolar and I fought it. I didn't want to take medications. I must take Medications to even out my moods. I didn't like any remarks about. It took me 30 years to find out to find the right medications. I had to be admitted to the hospital for depression. I didn't know what was wrong with me. I hurt so bad inside I totally didn't want to be mentally ill. I fought it tooth and nail. I didn't want to admit it. I didn't want to take my pills right. My husband and daughter went to the veterans. Clinic and asked why they couldn't do something to make be better. I went to my appointments and got treatment. Letting others know how I felt and their prayers have kept me going many people helped me. Clergy, counselors, doctors, and nurses as well as friends and family have all supported me. In recent years there has been more help to the two million people with mental problems. It's a chemical imbalance issue.

CHAPTER

3

There are holistic methods that help. These are extremely helpful methods. For those who seek relief from their unhappy conditions. But I have found my faith lifts me up and I don't get so bad any more. And I also know my Savior. Jesus has pleased God by dying for my sins and I have been blessed by God. I went to classes. I have found my faith lifts me up and I don't get so bad anymore. And I know my savior. Jesus has pleased God by dying for my sins and I have been blessed by God and he keeps me safe and protected and I pray for myself and others. There are success stories in Choices in Recovery, a periodical. There are "holistic" methods of recovery too. A book called Genuine Recovery has much truth in understanding so many of the lies we tell ourselves. This book is very good. It is a study of those with problems of heart and soul and mind. There are success stories in several of the classes I had to take. I had to go to jail at one point. That's how bad it was for me. I know now my Heavenly Father lovingly but sternly watch over me all the time. Sometimes it's rough but His work gives me confidence and it is very logical to study his word is a great tool for truth and love, hope and faith, healing, comforting. That's why I played my horn some. I got my lip back yesterday and want to play for my wonderful Savior. I depend on God to use his wonderful word and great love to guide me and protect me.

Many have bad experiences when they were children. There is nothing they can do an about it but accept it and forgive the perpetrator if possible. I am bipolar and I fought it. I didn't want to take my medicine. But I had to finally accept it I felt so much better when I take it. I depend on God and he keeps me safe and protected and I pray for myself and others. There is success stories in the Choices in Recovery Periodical listed in the bibliography at the end of this pamphlet. There are holistic methods of recovery too. In this method of recovery there are many descriptions and choices in action. These methods are based on God's truth. I have read a book of letters to a father, and the Bible for truth and love.

Glenn Close the Actress is helping her sister to overcome her being bipolar and they are writing a book. And Robin Williams succumbed to the problem. My husband and I believe he had a terrible accident that took his life. So sad.

He thought he had onset of Alzheimer's disease and his great depression made him so ill that he took his own life.

It is beautiful to see a parent support a Down's syndrome child and help him or her go on trips to the beauty parlor. Or to trips to the store or restaurant I've seen it when I was young in church. And for all times I've seen in when I was young, I was afraid of it and afraid for the child. But with love and encouragement and training they can have a beautiful life.

Here is some background on me. Don't get too bored before you give this to change you for the better.

This is a book about we who are always looking for meaning in their life. And always wondering if we do the right thing. It is a personal tragedy to those who are afflicted. One of the worst is when we think other people can read our minds. Another terrible experience is the black hole. That is a deep sick depression and it wants to quit. It is so terrible. God, please save us from that. Some people are intolerant of those who are in desperate need for someone to listen. They aren't well accepted by some. It might be a bum or a homeless person. Or it might be somebody who is hungry.

CHAPTER

4

We try to help them all You just don't know who is going to help them. Who trusts anybody in this selfish society? Maybe they are illiterate. Some are war veterans in need. There is always somebody who will help those in need. Let's hope! I don't say like to hear someone say, "go ahead and jump" to someone who is so close to jumping because it's just too tough for them to hold on to life. Most people don't seem to care.

I love to play my horn. Mom and Dad bought me two new horns for me to play. I practiced it every day almost and they encouraged me to play and I did love it. I still play it today. They really didn't have the money to buy me new trumpets. They even let me go to music camp in Indiana and Pennsylvania.

Two years. That's why I must play my trumpet. God has forgiven me for my waywardness and wandering. He even provided forgiveness to me and I forgive anyone who would try to do me harm. Some just don't have time for people who want to hurt people who are in bad circumstances. They need pills to help them through a rough trial period. I love to play my horn. I practiced it every day almost and they encouraged me to play and I did love it. I still play it today. They really didn't have the money to buy me new trumpets. They even let me go to music camp in Indiana and Pennsylvania. Two years. That's why I must play my trumpet. God has forgiven me for my waywardness and wandering. He even provided forgiveness to me and I forgive anyone who would try to do me harm. Some just don't have time for people who want to hurt people who are in bad circumstances. They need pills to help them through a rough trial period. I have had 38 jobs in about 13 years If I had been smart enough, I should have sung for this guitar player. He wanted to have a gig with playing his guitar and my singing and horn. He said his wife would understand. I should have taken him up on that. I learned that faith in the one and only Lamb of God and acceptance of so great a salvation through the blood of the one who takes our sins away can give us peace, confidence. Take fears away. He keeps working on us.

At the college in Indiana our Brass Choir Band toured Florida churches with our concerts Some Gracious people hosted us and let us stay overnight till the next day when we were at another church for a concert.

I practiced my horn in Jr. High school and High school and was in the band. I was first chair trumpet for a few years. Our marching band played at the "Indy 500" race car track that was pretty hard too. Playing our instruments in the festivities. My mother was so good to me. 'She bought me a new Conn trumpet for band. And later after a few years she bought me a trumpet called a Bach. A very good trumpet. I played it up even till now. I play in Church. On Sunday. I liked trumpet, I practiced almost every day. It was a challenge and I could do it. I had four brothers so I was comfortable playing sports with the boys in elementary school somewhat a tomboy. I played sports and music that was my young life that took up most of my time. Also, I went to church and played my horn there with the choir when I wasn't singing. Mom would be there in church. And she would smile so big. Our stage band played in the basketball season in school.

I didn't have many plans for my future so Mom talked to me about going to college, I went along with her. I was to go to Tennessee Temple College. I went there a year. I wrote my first poem there. And I Took Speech class there. Also, I played tennis there. I had some jobs. In the summer. I bought an English bike with the various speeds. I bought a 75cc Honda motorcycle to carry my trumpet on and went to Mary's.

· JULy · 69

She played the piano. And we practiced *Count Your Many Blessings* for a church contest and won a first place trophy being the best in that contest! When I went to church, I played my horn. Mom would smile so big. She taught me to sing alto for harmony. Mom had a big garden. She loved to get up in the early morning when I was cool out. I remembered so clearly that she wore pants in the garden. She always wore a dress other times. I didn't ask her but I'm sure she wore farmer's clothes when she helped Grandpa farm.

Then we snapped beans and pea podded. Mom washed her carrots and beets. I picked beans and ran the gas dirt tiller for weeds. She cooked and froze sweet corn, canned tomatoes, pears, and green beans. There was loose leaf lettuce, potatoes. I made chili at home.

Rhubarb, strawberries and sunflowers. Grandmother pickled apples and beets and they were good.

I remember swinging on the weeping willow tree. And we had rope and board swing in the pear tree.

We had a basketball hoop and backboard. We had about three acres and a big enough lot to hold horses. So, I built fence, the best I could. Our pinto, "Mary" bore a little foal called, "Queenie." She was so soft white and brown like her mother I went to college a year but didn't like being so far from home. So, I enrolled in Grace College in Warsaw Indiana. There I was in the brass choir. We went to Florida from Indiana and we played our instruments in several churches there. Some gracious hosts took me in their home so I could travel with the Brass Choir. My trumpet teacher there played a metal funnel instead of his trumpet. He played *Stars and Stripes Forever"* on that funnel. What a happy musician he was. I lived in a dormitory for women and had a few friends.

I woke up every day with my Baby Ben Alarm clock. Got dressed and went to breakfast. I went to College for 1 ½ years. Both religious colleges I got pretty good grades. I was losing my independence. I could not do anything all alone any more. I needed something else. So, I went home to my Mom.

I wanted to be with my mother. I wanted to learn from her and I wanted encouragement. But we didn't know I was bipolar.

Back in Indiana mom was exercising and losing weight. Dad said if she lost 50 pounds, he would put aluminum siding on the house. She did lose weight and Dad had the white aluminum siding put on. She went to her church to volunteer and crossing the intersection two guys were high on something and they shouldn't even have been driving. They ran a red light into the intersection just as mom was Crossing the bypass. They hit her front left. The engine was picked up off the road. My sister-in-law called and told me, "Drive up to the hospital quick your mom has been in a bad car accident." My brother and I drove to the hospital. He said, "Can we drive a little faster?" We were there in about 20 minutes. I was lost so depressed. God took her to heaven one month after I went home. We all suffered mom's loss. I couldn't cry. I could have been in the car with her. But I was too sad to go with her. She died in the emergency room where she was an admissions clerk in the hospital. I should have been there with her. I wish I could have held her hand and told her I loved her. I was almost totally lost. I was so unhappy. Dad couldn't keep me home. He did help get me a job at a family restaurant. A family diner just east of town called "Tote-a-poke." I washed pans and dishes. It was a nice family business. But I was hurting. The wound was festering. I was so unhappy and depressed. I didn't know what was wrong with me. I never felt good.

After some recuperation and I had money. I moved to Iowa where my aunt lived. My grandmother. Mom's mother. Let me stay with her upstairs. I'm afraid I was making a mess of my life. I had been Molested very early in life and really needed counseling I didn't know that even yet. I worked in a farm machinery and parts department store for farmers in Iowa. There I met, I thought a very good guy at work. Larry and I went out together.

I needed to get away from there I didn't have enough money to live. So, I joined the Navy so I could go back to school. I took Hospital Corp School in Florida...

The words of God are telling us that faith is the substance of things hoped for and the; evidence of things not seen. Through faith we understand that the worlds were framed by the words of God so that things which are seen were not made of things which do appear. This scripture is good because it tells us about faith and how real it is. It's pure logic. God knows what all things are made of. And all things are made of things we can't see with the naked eye. There are cells. Finely tuned body tissue and the human body is a miracle of God's creation. Everything that was made was made by God himself.

But without faith it is impossible to please Insert he that cometh to God must believe that he is and he is a rewarder of them that diligently seek him… I was always impressed by Christian music. One song is *In the image of God we were made long ago. I believed if we were made in the one selects image of God he knew mostly about me. So, I took comfort in that. I didn't know I needed anything else!? I could not believe I had a mental illness that was sapping the life out of me. It cost me plenty. The America I loved was who I wanted to be with. So, I joined the Navy. Then it started to happen. I needed to be 4.0 and I could not be that there, it was just too hard to cope. I was 12th in my class in my high school class. I spoke the prayer for my class commencement. But I was so miserable! Thank you, USA, for finding out what my problem was. But I didn't want to accept that. Now it's so easy to take my pills and get a shot. God, bring honor to this dear US of A. Which diagnosed me and helps me every day? I knew I loved my country. I always did.* I am so unhappy with this indecision, lack of leadership. The stage is set for a leader here in the USA. Don't you see the stage being set for these times?

He has a plan for your life. So, God could look upon us and love us, protect us and lead us. There was to be no other offering He died for all— unconditionally, and with no limits, or boundaries, color or race, or age. Still, He is the giver of life; not man. God has a wonderful plan for every baby's life. God has a plan for every baby's life. God loves little babies.

These Old-Testament believers all died in faith not having received the promises but having seen them afar off and were blessed with families and large herds of animals.

The sin which so easily beset us let us run with patience the race that is set before us looking unto Jesus the author and finisher of our faith; who for the joy that was set before him endured the cross despising the shame, and, and is set down at the right hand of the throne of GOD himself, lest ye be wearied and faint in your minds. You have not yet resisted unto blood striving against sin. We had faith in the one and only true God, and acceptance of so great a salvation through the blood of the one and only Lamb of God who is Jesus Christ our Lord and savior who takes the sin of the world away.

The Bible says this in the love chapter. There three things, faith hope and charity. The greatest of these is charity. Charity is love. There are several kinds of love. God's expression of love for us is that he put his son Named Jesus on earth to be born, grow, and be favorable with God and man who preach in parables and do what His father wanted him to do. His death was planned on a cruel cross. He preached and healed people. He had done the will of the Father and man grew so hateful towards him they crucified their only Savior. After his three years.

He died, rose to life again. Prepared his Disciples to continue his ministry here after he that he went to be with God the Father. And is sitting at the right hand of God. Praying for us. Jesus said, "Father Forgive them for they don't know what they are doing." He forgave his assailants and we should forgive people too.

God has a wonderful plan for your life. Those victims of mental diseases and emotional trauma and Injury; they wandered about being destitute, Afflicted and full of trauma, subject to demons and sickness of the mind and heart. These people need to have a chance just like anybody else. Only God the father knows their pain. I will confess I had a real bad trial with the dark side. But He found me and gradually brought me back through medication and the prayers of my friends and family. It hasn't been easy for them. And it hasn't been easy for me. But I'm not done yet. I will ask my Heavenly father for one more chance to share my books with others.

CHAPTER

5

Still, He is the Giver of life. Those were victims of mental diseases and emotional trauma and injury, subject to demons and sickness of mind and heart. These need to have a chance, God knows their pain and miraculously heals; it's true. Our Bible is our love letters from God himself the only one true creator. God sent his son for our salvation. When there is great trouble inside a person that person needs to hear the GOOD NEWS that there was a man on earth who had the power to overcome that. He loves the troubled soul. He removes the evil spirit from within him or her. Jesus came to earth to win victory for us. He came to heal the sick and lame and cause the blind man to see; raise the sick to health and bring back life to some who were dead.

He answered them who asked for help. The entire world could not contain the books that could be written of the things Jesus did in his life on earth. He knew he came to the world to die. He did what his father wanted him to do.

He healed forgave, cried, had sympathy for those who down and out. He brought back to life a young girl whose mother asked that she be brought back to life. Yes,

Jesus said the young girl was actually dead. He came by and spoke to the girl and she came back to life. Then there was Lazarus. Jesus was a friend of the family… Mary and Martha were the sisters. A complaint that if Jesus had been there sooner Lazarus would not have died. This brought emotional pain to Jesus. He cried, for he loved Lazarus and his family. Jesus said to them, "Oh ye who are of little faith why don't you trust me? Believe in me." For I am your every thing. There is only one way to heaven. Also there is a real hell. It's in black and white or red and white in the Bible. Jesus very words are in red and white in the New Testament. You have a door to your heart. Just open the door to your heart. You will be born again. No one else knows you like Jesus does. He was a man too. He had friends who were women. But he was without sin. We all have sinned and we know it. And people have sinned against us but we want to be sure the sin against us doesn't stop us from forgiving them and Jesus will bring a forgiving spirit to us peace to our hearts and minds.

Corinthians 13 New Testament
This is the Love Chapter

"Even if I speak with tongues of men and angels, and have not charity, I am become as sounding brass, or a tinkling cymbal. And though I have the gift of prophecy, and understand all mysteries, and all knowledge; and though I have all faith. So that I could remove mountains, and have not charity, I am nothing. There are these things, faith, hope, and charity. But the greatest of these is charity."

This is from the "love" chapter in the Bible. There are several kinds of Love. God's great love to send his son to us to make for us a way to heaven. There is man's love for one another as we are instructed to have compassion one of another. To find out and pray for our loved one's burdens. Charity suffers long and is kind; charity envied not; charity vaunted not itself, is not puffed up. It is practiced until it is a frame of mind. Please let me glean from the fields what is remaining which are overflowing and adequate for some time to come. As Ruth gleaned from Boaz's fields. And Boaz was smitten with Ruth. And made provisions for her in his fields.

The sin which so easily besets us? Let us run with patience the race that is set before us looking unto Jesus the author and finisher of our faith; who for the joy that was set before him endured the cross despising the shame, and is set down at the right hand of the throne of God himself, lest you be wearied and faint in your minds. You have not yet resisted unto blood striving against sin. They had faith in the one and only Lamb of God who is Jesus Christ our Lord and savior who takes the sin of the world away. The bible says this in the love chapter. Thee three things, faith, hope and charity. The greatest of these is charity. There are several kinds of love. God's expression of love for us is that he put his son Named Jesus on earth to be born, grow and be favorable with God and man who is sitting at the right hand throne of God. Praying for us.

CHAPTER

6

Those Old-Testament believers all died in faith not having received the promises but having seen them afar off and were blessed with families and large herds of animals. They were persuaded of those promises of God and embraced them and confessed that they were strangers and pilgrims on the earth.

God has a wonderful plan for your life. Those victims of mental diseases and emotional trauma and injury. Some wandered about being destitute, afflicted and full of trauma, subject to demons and injury they wandered about being destitute. Afflicted and full of trauma. Subject to demons and sickness of the mind and heart. These people need to have a chance just like anybody else. God knows their pain.

Jesus is sitting at the right hand side of the Father God. Jesus said forgive them for they don't know what they do when he was crucified on the cross. Jesus forgave his killers and we have to try to forgive those who have mistreated us. Jesus said, "Father forgives them for they knew not what they did." We who have endured a lot should at some point forgive our enemies.

I will confess I had a real bad trial with the dark side. But He found me. The Father knew my pain. He found me and gradually brought me back through medication and the prayers of my friends and family. I HAD TO LEARN TO PRAY. I'm not done yet. As long as I have breath and God grants me forgiveness and breath. I will continue on. I will ask my Heavenly Father for one more chance to share my books with others.

When there is great trouble inside a person, they need to hear the GOOD NEWS that there was a man on earth who understood and has the power to overcome that. He loves the troubled soul. He removes the pain and fear. Jesus came to earth to win victory for us. He came to earth to heal the sick and the lame. The Blind man to see. Bring back to health some who were dead. He answered those who asked for help. The entire world could not contain the books that could be written about the work and healing teaching and ministering for people in his 3 years of ministry. He did what his Father wanted him to do. He healed, forgave, cried, and had sympathy for those who are down and out. A mother had a young daughter who had an unclean spirit in her daughter. Jesus told the spirit to leave her. And the spirit left her.

Then there was Lazarus. Jesus was a friend of the family. Mary and Martha were the sisters. A complaint that if Jesus had been there sooner Lazarus would not have died. This brought emotional pain to Jesus. He cried, for he loved Lazarus and his family. Jesus said to them, "Oh ye who are of little faith why don't you trust me? Believe in me. For I am your everything." There is only one way to heaven. Also, there is a real hell. It's in black and white in the bible. Jesus' words sometimes are in red. You have a door to your heart. Just open the door to your heart. Invite Jesus into your heart. You will be born again. No one knows you like Jesus does. He was a man too. He had friends who were women. But he was without sin. We all have sinned and we know it. And people have sinned against us but we want to be sure the sin against us doesn't stop us from forgiving them and Jesus will bring a forgiving spirit to us and peace to our hearts and minds.

CHAPTER

7

Noah Genesis 6

Noah moved for the loving respect and fear of God and built an ark in the desert so his family wouldn't drown God showed the animals the way to the ark two by two. (Except for the rabbits and they were a little problem because they wanted to multiply faster That is a contribution of my husband.)

It rained for 40 days and nights upon the earth and everything drowned upon the earth even the bad people, and the ones that laughed at Noah perished. God covered the whole earth when he sent the flood. Can you pause and ponder; how did the Grand Canyon become so awesome! How else can you explain it? A tremendous torrent of water accumulating on earth. Continents were formed at one stage, at creation or from the flood. The earth hadn't had rain like this until the flood.

Abraham went out into a strange place by faith in God. He went out to a strange land. He was looking for a city which hath foundations whose builder and maker is God. He had Isaac and Jacob with him of the same promise. Also, through faith Sarah received strength to conceive seed, and was delivered of a child when she was past age, because she judged him faithful who had promised. Abraham believed God's promise by faith. He was to be the father of a great nation, God's people.

There sprang as many as the stars of the sky in multitude, and is as the sand by the seashore innumerable. All of these old testament believers died desiring a better country that was heavenly.

Genesis

Now we want to go back to Cain and Able, the first brothers, sons of Adam and Eve. Oh let's see how Cain and able did as God visited them and their offerings.

Cain grew vegetation for man and animals. He was a tiller of the soil. Able was the animal farmer. God required animal sacrifice. Evidently Cain did not want to ask his brother for a sacrifice. God only accepted an animal sacrifice. Cain had words with Able. Cain wanted to please God but he knew his plants weren't enough for offering. The two boys spoke and Cain rose up against his brother in the field and slew him. God couldn't accept Cain's offering of vegetables and plants.

Cain was very upset and afraid of punishment from God, Cain said, "I will be a vagabond and every man that finds me will want to kill me."

The Lord said, "Anyone who slays Cain had better not because the Lord set a mark upon Cain so any finding him would not kill him for if they did vengeance on him would be seven fold."

God spoke to the fathers in the past by the prophets— The old Testament Patriarchs of God. In these last days he spoke to us by his son whom he hath appointed heir of all things, by whom also God made the world. Jesus the brightness of his glory, and the express image of His person, purged our sins, sat down on the right hand of the Majesty on high. Think about that for a while. Even the angels knew His inheritance, a more excellent name than they. Let all of the angels worship him.

Abraham went out into a strange place by faith in God. He went out to a strange land. He was looking for a city which hath foundations whose builder and maker is God. He had Isaac and Jacob with him of the same promise. Also, through faith Sarah received strength to conceive a seed and had baby Isaac, and was delivered of a child when she was past age, because she judged him faithful who had promised. Abraham believed God's promise by faith. He was to be the father of a great nation, God's people.

There sprang as many as the stars of the sky in multitude, and is as the sand by the seashore innumerable. All of these old testament believers died desiring a better country that was heavenly: where fore God is not ashamed to be called their God: for he hath prepared for them a city.

CHAPTER

8

I mean these men Abraham, Moses, Jacob, Esau, Isaac, Joseph and Moses all by faith desired a better country. Read more in Hebrews Chapter 10 New Testament: the BIBLE.

The Old Testament Patriarchs of God. In these last days spoke to us by his son whom he hath appointed heirs of all things, by whom also he. God, made the worlds. Jesus who being the brightness of his glory, and the express image of his person. Purged our sins, sat down on the right had of the Majesty on high. Think about that for a while. Even the angels knew his inheritance, a more excellent name than they. Let all of the angels worship him.

A sacrifice of a burnt bull and of goats would not take sins away, when Jesus came into the world, he said sacrifice and offering would not, but a body has thou prepared me: Then Jesus said, "Lo, I come in volume of a book it is written of me, to do thy will, O God." And every priest stands daily ministering and offering often times the same sacrifices, which can never take away sins; but Jesus' body and spilt blood is your sacrifice This is the covenant that I will make with them after those days, saith the Lord, I will put my laws into their hearts. And in their minds will I write them; and their sins and iniquities I will remember no more. There is no more offering for Sin. Let us draw near with a true Heart in full assurance of faith having our hearts sprinkled from an evil conscience, and our bodies washed with pure water. Let us hold fast the profession of our faith without wavering; for he is faithful having our hearts. Sprinkled from an evil conscience, and our and let us consider one another to provoke unto love and to good works. Not forsaking the assembling of ourselves together let us hold fast the profession of faith one another; and to much the more as you see the day approaching when he will return to take us with him to heaven.

CHAPTER

9

Deuteronomy Chapter 5
THE TEN COMMANDMENTS

1. THOU SHALL HAVE NO OTHER GODS BEFORE ME.

2. THOU SHALL NOT MAKE THEE ANY GRAVEN IMAGE, LIKENESS OF ANYTHING IN HEAVEN ABOVE OR THAT THAT I THE EARTH, OR WATERS BENEATH THE EARTH.

3. THOU SHALL NOT TAKE THE NAME OF THE LORD THY GO VAIN; FOR THE LORD WILL NOT HOLD HIM GUILTLESS T TAKETH HIS NAME IN VAIN.

4. KEEP THE SABBETH DAY TO SANCTIFY IT, AS THE LORD HAD COMMANDED THEE. SIX DAYS SHALL THOU LABOR DO ALL THY WORK.

5. HONOR THY FATHER AND MOTHER AS THE LORD AS THE L COMMANDED THEE THAT

IT MAY GO WELL WITH THEE. IN LAND WHICH THE LORD THY GOD GIVETH THEE.

6. THOU SHALT NOT KILL.

7. NEITHER SHALL THOU COMMIT ADULTERY.

8. NEITHER SHALL THOU STEAL.

9. NEITHER SHALL THOU BEAR FALSE WITNESS AGAINST NEIGHBOR.

10. NEITHER SHALL THOU DESIRE THY NEIGHBOR'S WIFE, NEIT HIS FIELD, OR HIS MAN SERVANT OR HIS MAID SERVANT, HIS OR HIS ASS OR ANYTHING OR ANYTHING THAT IS NEIGHBOR'S.

These words the Lord spoke to Moses unto all his assembly in the mount out of the midst of the fire, of the cloud, and of the thick darkness, with a great voice and he added no more and he wrote them in two tablets of stone and delivered them to Moses. Do these commandments and keep them. These are written for God's people. Abraham and his descendants to be numbered as the stars in the sky and the sand underfoot.

John 3:16,17

FOR GOD SO LOVED THE WORLD THAT HE GAVE HIS ONLY BEGOTTON SON THAT WHOSOEVER BELIEVED IN HIM SHOULD NOT PERISH BUT HAVE EVERLASTING LIFE. FOR GOD SENT NOT HIS SON INTO THE WORLD

TO CONDEMN THE WORLD BUT THAT THE WORLD THROUGH HIM MIGHT BE SAVED!

So, Jesus gave his life for God's people and He also gave his life for everybody. No matter what nationality they were of what previous beliefs they had, or what their parents believed which can never take away sins; but his man after he had offered one sacrifice for sins forever, sat down at the right hand of God. No one fully realizes the horrible suffering of Jesus for us. If you have suffered, you are closer to Jesus than you realize!

CHAPTER

10

Hebrews 4: 12

For the word of God is quick and powerful
And sharper than any two edged sword,
Piercing even to the dividing asunder of the
Soul and spirit and of the joints and marrow.

They run the race and it's no lark.
Holding fast to Christ the rock.
Keep praying for the discernment of the thoughts and
intents of the heart.

Let us labor wherefore to enter into that rest,
Lest you fall after the same example of unbelief.
We must remind ourselves that without faith it is
impossible to.

Please God and to heal us, for he that comes to God must
believe that He is a rewarder of them that diligently seek
him. Many, many before us lived by faith.
When you have an on going illness that never get better
like ours, God has provided relief.
And laughter is good for the soul. AMEN

Do these commandments and keep them. These are written for God's people.

I spent 3 months of my life searching in my mind for the answer to any problem or question I had. My Doctor said it was a waste of time. But it proved something to me. But I had to satisfy my own self. I found out for myself that God was all in all. Everything goes in a cycle of truths and untruths. myself that God was all in all. Too. But the essence of living day to day is to pray, in prayer for those to seek for the good. Because every good thing comes from God. In Lakeland, FL a chaplain in a hospital was unseated for praying in Jesus' Name "Amen." I think Christians should speak up for their beliefs. Her has been too much damage to our Christian heritage. And our children's freedom to believe by hearing the truth. Freedom was stolen by taking prayer, Bibles and the pledge of allegiance out of schools all across this land in public schools.

IN JESUS' NAME

When the Chaplain Bowed to pray
Some didn't like it and had the nerve to say so.
When they press toward the mark
Men and women who are keeping
Our freedom from oppression.
Their families are so far away.
How do they get by?
When we kneel our prayers to say,
"Keep them father out of harms' way."
Let them pray in Jesus's Name
Or we should all be put to shame.

BIBLIOGRAPHY

CHOICES IN RECOVERY, PERIODICAL WITH SUCCESS STORIES

Support and information for Schizophrenia, and bipolar disorder

GENUINE RECOVERY

Recover's guide to true inner healing renewal of the mind. Edward M. Smith

THE BIBLE THE KING JAMES VERSION

God's Holy BIBLE for reference.
www.thebetterwaybooks.com

Other books by Lois E. Lund:

Baby Chick
Faith in Action